If you were an

Adverb

by Michael Dahl
illustrated by Sara Gray

WITHDRAWN

PICTURE WINDOW BOOKS
Minneapolis, Minnesota

adverb (adv) a word that describes or modifies a verb, an adjective, or another adverb

Editor: Christianne Jones
Designer: Nathan Gassman
Page Production: Tracy Kaehler
Creative Director: Keith Griffin
Editorial Director: Carol Jones
The illustrations in this book
were created with acrylics.

Picture Window Books
151 Good Counsel Drive
P.O. Box 669
Mankato, MN 56002-0669
877-845-8392
www.picturewindowbooks.com

Printed in the United States
of America.

All books published by Picture Window
Books are manufactured with paper
containing at least 10 percent
post-consumer waste.

Special thanks to our advisers for
their expertise:

Rosemary G. Palmer, Ph.D.
Department of Literacy, College of Education
Boise State University

Susan Kesselring, M.A., Literacy Educator
Rosemount—Apple Valley—Eagan
(Minnesota) School District

Library of Congress Cataloging-in-Publication Data
Dahl, Michael.
If you were an adverb / written by Michael Dahl ;
illustrated by Sara Gray.
p. cm. — (Word fun)
Includes bibliographical references and index.
ISBN 978-1-4048-1357-1 (hardcover)
ISBN 978-1-4048-1983-2 (paperback)
1. English language—Adverb—Juvenile literature.
I. Gray, Sara, ill. II. Title. III. Series.
PE1325.D34 2006
428.2—dc22
2005021857

Looking for adverbs? Watch for the big, colorful words in the example sentences.

If you were
an adverb ...

Like peanut butter and jelly,
verbs and adverbs go
well together.

If you were an adverb, you would work closely with verbs.

7

Verbs tell us something happened. If you were an adverb, you could tell us how something happened.

The snowboarder skied GRACEFULLY down the mountainside,

but he fell **AWKWARDLY** at the bottom.

9

If you were an adverb, you might have a tail. Many adverbs end in the letters "ly."

How did the bear dive?

CLUMSILY

PERFECTLY

SPEEDILY

The volleyball player hit the ball **SHARPLY** and **POWERFULLY.** A player on the other side jumped **FEARLESSLY** into the air.

If you were an adverb, you would work at the beginning, the middle, or the end of a sentence.

RAPIDLY, the runner rounded the curve.

The runner **RAPIDLY** rounded the curve.

The runner rounded the curve **RAPIDLY.**

If you were an adverb, you could tell us how often something happens.

The long jumper **ALWAYS** jumps

The long jumper OFTEN jumps

14

more than 20 feet (6 meters).

more than 28 feet (8.5 meters).

If you were an adverb, you could tell us when something is going to happen. You could be something NOW, LATER, TODAY, TOMORROW, or YESTERDAY.

Some teams will play NOW.

Other teams will play LATER.

17

If you were an adverb,
you could help adjectives
describe things better.

Some athletes
are **VERY** tall.

Some athletes are
SOMEWHAT short.

Some athletes are **IMMENSELY** muscular.

Some athletes are **EXTRAORDINARILY** fast.

Some athletes are **TOO** busy practicing.

If you were an adverb,
you could modify
other adverbs.

The crowd watches **VERY CLOSELY** as the athletes

compete EXTREMELY WELL.

You would put together super sentences ...

... if you were an adverb!

The ADVERB GAME

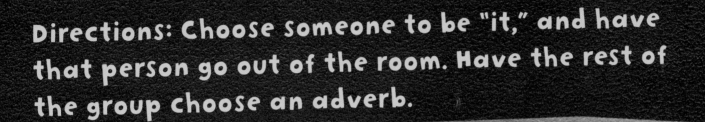

Directions: Choose someone to be "it," and have that person go out of the room. Have the rest of the group choose an adverb.

Call your friend back into the room. Have your friend pick someone in the group to act out the adverb. For example, "Walk across the room like the adverb."

Your friend must watch for clues and then guess what the adverb is. Do they move swiftly or dreamily or spookily?

Your friend can pick up to three different people to act out the adverb in different ways. After three chances, explain what the adverb was, choose another person from the group to be "it," and start over.

Fact: If you look up an adverb in the dictionary, you will see the abbreviation "adv" next to it. The "adv" stands for adverb.

Glossary

awkwardly—doing something in a clumsy way
clumsily—doing something in a way that lacks grace
eagerly—wanting to do something very much
energetically—using lots of energy to do something
extraordinarily—doing something in a remarkable way
fearlessly—showing no fear
gracefully—doing something in a smooth manner
immensely—of great size
modify—to change in some way

To Learn More

At the Library

Cleary, Brian P. Dearly, Nearly, Insincerely: What Is an Adverb? Minneapolis: Carolrhoda Books, 2003.
Heinrichs, Ann. Adverbs. Chanhassen, Minn.: Child's World, 2004.
Heller, Ruth. Up, Up, and Away: A Book About Adverbs. New York: Grosset & Dunlap, 1991.

On the Web

FactHound offers a safe, fun way to find Web sites related to this book. All of the sites on FactHound have been researched by our staff.

1. Visit www.facthound.com
2. Type in this special code: 1404813578
3. Click on the FETCH IT button.

www.FactHound.com

Your trusty FactHound will fetch the best sites for you!

Index

Look for all of the books in the Word Fun series:

If You Were a Noun
If You Were a Verb
If You Were an Adjective
If You Were an Adverb
If You Were a Conjunction
If You Were an Interjection
If You Were a Preposition
If You Were a Pronoun
If You Were an Antonym
If You Were a Homonym or a Homophone
If You Were a Palindrome
If You Were a Synonym